Getting That First Job or Internship In Finance

Proven steps to launching your career with help from an insider

Wayne Walker

© Copyright 2019 by Wayne Walker, All rights reserved.

This book was written with the goal of providing information that is as accurate and reliable as possible. Professionals should be consulted as needed before undertaking any of the actions endorsed herein.

This declaration is deemed fair and valid by both the American Bar Association and the Committee of Publishers Association and is legally binding throughout the United States.

Furthermore, the transmission, duplication or reproduction of any of the following work, including precise information, will be considered an illegal act, irrespective whether it is done electronically or in print. The legality extends to creating a secondary or tertiary copy of the work or a recorded copy and is only allowed with express written consent of the Publisher. All additional rights are reserved.

The information in the following pages is broadly considered to be a truthful and accurate account of facts, and as such any inattention, use or misuse of the information in question by the reader will render any resulting actions solely under their purview. There are no scenarios in which the publisher or the author of this work can be in any fashion deemed liable for any hardship or damages that may befall them after undertaking information described herein.

Table of Contents

Introduction: Why this book? 5
We begin by getting to the point 7
Getting this network on campus 11
Finance career paths & the impact of technology 17
Resume or CV? 21
The interview 25
Some notes on phone or online interviews 29
The job offer 31
Negotiating the salary 33
Making the most of the internship or student job 36
The first job after graduation 41
The social scene 45
The GCMS Finance Assessment Exercise 48
Finance candidate interview questions 55
Resources 63
Conclusion 65
Profile of The Author 67

Introduction: Why this book?

The question that must be answered for any book of this type is, why? What's the point? Am I just filling the pages with words, or is there some clear value that will be provided to the readers. I will skip the suspense. I believe this book accomplishes the goal of delivering value in as many pages that are needed but without excess (my other books are known for getting to the point).

In the following pages, I will share, in straight talk, what is needed to open the doors to a job or career in finance. The straight talk is coming from my personal experience of working in the banking and finance sectors across several countries and continents. Most important for readers are the ideas that I have shared with students and recent graduates globally. These ideas and tips have been used with successful outcomes. In plain terms, this is the book that I wished was available when I graduated from university. My suggestions have worked for thousands, BUT I am not arrogant enough to suggest perfection, as anything or anyone can be improved.

We begin by getting to the point

The bottom line in securing the job once you have an interview is convincing the interviewers that you will help them reach their goals better than any other candidate. Please think about this carefully…. you need to convince them that you are the best candidate to help them reach <u>their</u> goals. So important that it must be repeated. Try to imagine the scenario where the roles are reversed. Isn't this what you would also want from a candidate? The answer should be a clear yes!

Your task then is to find out as much as possible about the goals of the department or manager that will conduct the interview or interviews. Thankfully, we live in the age of the internet where an ocean of information is available for free or almost free. You will research there to get as much relevant information as possible. If you already know someone at the firm, then you have the ideal secret weapon to deploy in the battle.

What really matters

The previous paragraph relates to the interview. Now, we will examine some of the steps taken to secure that interview. The most important is your professional network of people you know and who *they know*. I really wish there was some magical way around this fact. If you do not read another sentence in this book, just get this point and you are halfway to your goal. This is unfair and I guess politically incorrect, but I don't have time for that and neither do you. Your connections will play an exaggerated role at the start of your career, fortunately or unfortunately, and they will follow you.

Before getting deeper into this, I must make clear that obviously your grades and the reputation of the school that you attended play a role, <u>but</u> a good network of connections beats them every time….with ease.

GETTING THAT FIRST JOB OR INTERNSHIP IN FINANCE

I begin by using myself as an example, and I will share examples of students that I have taught from across the globe, Europe, Asia, USA, etc. The common link to a majority of their successes or challenges in securing that initial job is their network.

My journey: Getting my first job in New York City had influence from the people that I knew in the industry. The first banking jobs that I was able to land in Europe were from tips that friends gave me. So good were the tips that one of the jobs was one of the "no interview" interview situations that becomes more common after your first few jobs. This "no interview" means that, instead of a traditional interview, you simply discuss whether there is a meeting of the minds between you and your potential employer.

Was my situation unique? Absolutely not! I can refer to an international career night speaker panel that I sat on a few years ago. On the panel, we all had an opportunity to describe briefly the process of how we got our jobs. The majority were in positions due to the "no interview" interview. To secure their positions, they basically had a discussion with someone they already knew from their network.

Now the cynic may think, well Wayne, that is okay for you and other seasoned professionals, but what about us students? Even if you agree with what I wrote in principle, you might ask what you can offer as "just a student." My view is that anyone who undervalues networking with a university student is missing out on many opportunities. The results for my firm through the "just a student" connections have been fantastic. From international deals to online education partners, private clients, etc., the list is very long.

Some pointers: As a student, you DO have something to offer. You are in the know, in many cases, of the newest technology and trends, which is a valuable commodity. Another key point is that you will graduate; therefore, your situation and possibilities will change. Even as a student, your existing network is likely more valuable than you would believe. Any intelligent professional or firm should be aware that students don't just drop from the sky. You can never be sure of who are the friends, parents, or relatives of these students.

Bottom Line

From my real-world experience of dealing with finance students globally, the bottom line with securing the majority of their jobs had to do with someone in their network, and in some cases, it was me sharing my network with some of them.

Getting this network on campus

It would be a letdown to make a big deal about the role of your network without offering some steps on how to acquire one. As a student, your first moves begin on campus. Join whatever finance group or club that interests you as quickly as you can. The end goal being that you begin the process of building a professional network. Sure, you will learn many new things, but in the end, your expanded network is the goal. For example, in Europe, some student clubs are very popular and professional. I have worked with many of them. At the University of Groningen in the Netherlands, for example, the club leaders are out of school for the time that they lead the club. In other words, it is a full time job. That is how serious the groups can be.

The different clubs arrange practical classes about various topics, some that I have taught. They also have company nights. A company night is when banks, etc. have dinners where students can meet the staff and network themselves to summer internships and first jobs. Many, but not all, of these networking nights have a grade point average threshold; therefore, you will need good grades to participate.

Leadership

Now that you are in the group, the next step is to move beyond being a faceless member; stick your neck out and apply for a leadership position. This will provide you the opportunity to practice leading in the safe environment of school. If you make a mistake, so what? All is forgiven because you are a student. Better to make business mistakes in the safe environment of school and not in your professional life.

In many cases, your public speaking skills will improve dramatically. A note on public speaking, practice this skill as often as you can, one of the best ROI's of your time in school.

Ok, back to leadership. With a leadership role, you can maximize and turbocharge your networking opportunities. You will be the point of contact for all outside firms and partners. This could also lead to networking with other business or finance clubs at other universities to expand your network even more! Obviously, it looks good on your resume/CV, and it helps you to stand out in the often-crowded field of competitors.

Hands-on

Either as a club member or not, as soon and as much as possible, secure practical training in whatever area of finance that appeals to you. The more hands-on the training, the better. Remember, at university, you will get tons of theory; therefore, in your free time, no more theory is needed. The hands-on skills help to make you stand out in the selection process for internships or jobs. Another plus of these practical classes is that you get to connect with likeminded students, and you can help each other in the process.

LinkedIn

Create and maintain a LinkedIn account as soon as possible. This is the preferred tool for finance and business networking. Skip the profile photo of you at a beer-drinking contest and add one of you as a person on their way forward in life. From there, you can begin connecting to people in firms that interest you, especially alumni from your university. A note of caution, connecting to someone and then the next day begging for favors is considered very bad taste. The person will likely ban or ignore you. Another point in the networking journey is to begin the process <u>long</u> before you need to use it.

What to study?

One popular question that I get from students is: "How important is my major?" The quick answer is it matters, but it is not a deal breaker. As long as there is a base of classes that includes a mix of economics, finance, statistics, etc., then you are good. From my days on the hiring side of the desk, I have hired history majors; the most important for me was the person's interest and attitude. Having a strong finance background also does NOT hurt. Many firms and banks have their own training program, and they will teach you a lot of what you need to know.

To be realistic, the history or English major will increase their chances by having an internship at a bank or having a demo trading account as evidence of their interest, for example in trading. Also if you have a specific goal to be an accountant, then no surprise, your classes will have a heavy focus on that subject.

Cryptocurrencies and blockchain

At the time of writing, cryptocurrencies and blockchain technology are with us. Both are still relatively new, and it is recommended that you learn and understand the fundamental principles of them. For the unaware, blockchain is the underlying technology for cryptocurrencies. This is not an opinion piece on the technology; however, if you are advising clients, even if you do not personally like a product, you may still be required to be aware of it.

Languages

Outside business classes, one thing you should consider going heavy on is your language skills. This is probably more for students in the

United States, whose foreign language skills, generally, are not as strong as Europeans and others. The overwhelming majority of the students that I teach in Europe have fluency or near fluency in a minimum of 2 to 3 languages, students from the United States not so much. The more languages, the more opportunities for you; it is that simple.

The languages with a proven return on investment? English is the winner, as many call it the language of money. Arabic, Russian, German, or Mandarin are also your tickets to big bonuses if you are working on a trading team, private wealth management, and related areas. Yes, many of these clients speak English, but like other people in the world, they prefer to do business in their native language, especially when it involves their <u>money</u>.

From my years of experience managing foreign currency traders, the Middle East, Russian, and Asian teams had great trading volumes. Their clients like activity, and this is good for the team's bonus. For wealth management teams, a lot of the new wealth in the world is coming from the emerging markets; therefore, knowing their languages is a plus.

Your school's reputation

Your school's reputation is important, but it is <u>not</u> as important as some will try to make it out to be. You go to the school that works for you in the sense that you feel comfortable there. As people often say, "Go where you are celebrated and not just tolerated." Spending 3 to 6 years at a place you hate does not sound that appealing. Your school's reputation will play a role in the decision of a bank or firm that might want to visit for a career night or day. However, if you have been building your contacts during your time in university, then your school's reputation will still come in second or third place in terms of the importance in landing a job.

Finance career paths & the impact of technology

Where to begin your career in finance? A lot of it depends on your interest. The more outgoing personality might enter sales, and the more cerebral might get into options or algorithmic trading. It is important to keep in mind that a lot of the positions are specialized; therefore, once you are in, you are really in.

Investment Banking

These are some of the jobs that you often see in the movies. Action, glamour, money, and long hours. Where you end up, again, depends on your interest and aptitude. You can be on a trading desk executing forex or options trades. It could also include giving trading advice to high-net-worth individuals and corporations. Many investment banking firms are divided into divisions and regions. This also provides many opportunities to go international if that is a wish.

Commercial Banking

Commercial banking is what most people are familiar with when you mention banking. This could include your local bank for loans and mortgages. This is where you go if you prefer the local feel as a branch manager or a loan officer, etc.

Financial Planning

Financial planners and private wealth managers work with private clients to plan the best way to meet the client's financial goals. This could include tax planning or investment strategies to name just a few.

Private Equity

Private equity teams work with finding capital for firms, for example, a regional or global expansion. They can also be involved with corporate restructures or buyouts.

Corporate Finance

Corporate finance could involve working with mergers and acquisitions, prepping financial statements, or dealing with outside auditors.

Hedge Funds

Hedge funds are private investment funds where the managers have a lot of freedom in how and what they invest or trade. They can use leverage, derivatives, along with shorting the market. The jobs are considered hot, and no surprise, the competition is intense. Possible hedge fund positions include traders, portfolio managers, quantitative analyst, etc.

Prepping for the future (The impact of technology)

Finance is one area that has been impacted and will continue to be impacted by technology. It would be a disservice to you if we ignored or overlooked this topic.

When I started in finance, the tech guys were usually only seen as an expense at the bank where I worked. In recent years, there has been a noticeable mental shift in the industry, to where they are now part of the front office (where the money is made). Quants and programmers are now expected to be on the team to increase revenues.

First, you have algorithmic trading (algos), which is a **method of executing trades using automated pre-programmed trading instructions taking into account variables such as price, time, and volume.** This is sometimes referred to as black box trading.
Besides executing huge trades, algos can price assets faster than humans, which can be a threat to some options or bonds teams.

Next, are the robo-advisors. This is where banking clients can get financial advice or trading information with little to no human interaction. The advisors are run by algorithms.

Impact on jobs

As for the impact on the role of bankers and finance specialists, it simply means having basic skills from now on will *not* be enough. You will need to get extra training outside of what is typically offered in many universities. For example, programming skills: MQL4, Python, or C++. In the reference section of this book, there are suggested books that can help you further on these topics.

What astute professionals also see as the near-term influence of the new technologies is there will be less focus or time spent on routine tasks. Another way to view it is that technology will <u>not</u> eliminate traders or wealth managers; instead, it will actually allow them to perform at a higher level and become more productive. For example, with A.I. (Artificial Intelligence) unleashed, you can identify your underperforming clients faster or be alerted to overlooked investing opportunities.

Resume or CV?

First, a little on the differences. The noticeable differences are in the length and purpose. A resume is a brief snapshot of your skills and experience, and a CV is more detailed. Your resume is usually a page or maximum two pages long. A CV, in theory, could run four to six pages. Where you are in the world will determine what is best for you. In the United States, a resume is more common; for Europe, Asia, and the Middle East, a CV is the norm.

Whatever format you choose, I suggest you keep it to maximum two pages and lead with what is most relevant for the position that you are applying. As a person that has done a good amount of interviewing and hiring, I can tell you that I rarely read beyond a page or two. I was simply too busy, like many other managers and region leaders. We just wanted to get to the point, which is, can you help us achieve our goals?

You will include the basics; your name, address, etc. In Europe, especially in Northern Europe, many people include their date of birth along with a photo. Depending on your country, photos and dates of birth might be considered over the top. Besides the mentioned basics, you will highlight whatever paid or unpaid activity that you have done that is relevant to the position.

A few words about your less than glamorous positions. If you worked as a waiter, maid, etc. while in school, feel free to mention it. These positions show work ethic just as well as any other. Keep in mind, the people doing the interviews also had a wide range of jobs in university. The summer job that I had before starting university included cutting lawns in the boiling sun! There was never a problem finding jobs because of it. Later in life, I was even an "extra" or a supporting cast member at the Danish Royal Opera. I am not applying for jobs anymore, but when people contact me to consult on projects or for career coaching, to my surprise, one of the first things people ask me about is that job. Any place that will not hire you only because you cleaned rooms, probably are people that you do not want to spend too much time with. Remember that you are interviewing the firm just as much as they are interviewing you.

Unsolicited CV's

If you believe a company has irresistible opportunities for your future, then there is no need to wait until there is an official opening. If they believe your value propositions for helping them achieve their goals are valid, doors will open. At the very least, you will be the go-to person the minute there is an opening. Your initiative of taking a step forward has no downsides.

Applicant Tracking Systems

Let us review the technology that many of you will be up against in the job hunt. It is almost common practice now for large firms across many industries to deploy Applicant Tracking Systems (ATS), and the finance world is no different. These systems function by scanning CV's and resumes for keywords and phrases. In theory, this will ensure that only the best qualified candidates move forward in the job search process. Unfortunately, this is not always the case.

I now only wonder how many qualified people have been overlooked simply because they did not stack their resumes with enough keywords. Hopefully, this will finally drive home the point about having a network. If your network is strong enough, in many cases, you can skip this step.

Cover letter

Your cover letter is another important step in the job hunt. Here, your goal is to get the reader interested enough to give your CV a second look and hopefully invite you in for an interview. You will want to include why you are interested in the position and why they should invite you in for that interview.

The interview

Now you are finally at the crucial moment. If you have made it to the interview, then your chances of landing the job are reasonably good. If they thought that you had no chance, you would not have made it this far.

The key to succeeding in the interview is preparation. You are prepared when you know about the firm, where they are, and where they are looking to be. Then you get more granular. You will find out the role of the department that you are interviewing for in the big picture of the firm. You always want to keep in mind what motivates the other side (the interviewer). The preparation process will also include as much practice as possible in answering common interview questions. This will help to give you a more polished presentation. A collection of these sample questions is in a later chapter.

As mentioned, you must convince the interviewer that you are the best person to help them achieve their goals. You achieve this by projecting the image of confidence, and you will get this confidence by being prepared. Many studies reveal that the decision concerning if you capture the position or not is made within the first five minutes; therefore, your confident energy must be felt by all in the room.

You, as a rule, will listen more than you talk, but you will also want to have a list of questions about the position and the firm when they ask if you have any questions. Not having any questions when you get to this portion of the interview is not good. For example, your question could be getting more information about the typical career progression of someone who has the position that you are applying for.

My bottom line for interviews

The critical thing that I looked for when doing interviews was whether or not there was a match between the CV and the person that I saw in front of me. If any candidate told me "I have a passion" but showed no evidence of it, then things usually did not go well. If you have a "passion for trading," I better see lots of evidence, for example extra training or classes that you took outside of what was mandatory for your degree. Were you a member of a finance club? Did you have a demo trading account? These things bring alignment between the CV and the person.

WAYNE WALKER

Some notes on phone or online interviews

Many people ask me about how to tackle a phone interview. Phone or online interviews are common nowadays, so a strategy is needed. The good news is that you will use most of the suggestions that we have covered for the in-person interview. However, your listening skills will have to come up a level due to the fact that you are unable to see the interviewer.

Preparation is key, just as with the in-person interview. You will need a quiet area, free from any TV, background, or street noise to conduct the call. A writing pad or notebook of some kind is another must have. This is essential for taking notes of any numbers or key facts discussed that you would like to refer to later in the call. This also avoids you needing to ask for things to be repeated, and you present a more polished impression to the interviewer.

Many people, including myself, seem to perform better in these types of interviews while standing. Another tip that has worked for many is to dress as if or almost as if you are at an in-person interview. You read correctly. You dress as if you are there. It has been proven to provide a mental boost, in the same way that how you dress for many other areas in your life can influence how you act or perform.

A tip from my many years of public speaking that should provide an extra edge for you; prior to the interview, you should drink a good amount of water to have your throat lubricated. There is no need to go overboard, just a few glasses before and then a glass or bottled water on the side for during the interview.

If you are doing an online interview, then the obvious is that you must have a robust internet connection, and all your tech gadgets should be fully charged and tested <u>before</u> the interview.

The job offer

Good news! You have the offer that you have worked so hard for. The first step is to make sure the basics are correct; the position and salary are what you had in mind. Depending on the position, the offer will be done both by phone and then followed up with either mail or email. You will correct any discrepancies immediately and then move on to the next steps. For those that are unsure, please be aware that a job offer and acceptance by phone is legally binding.

Carefully review if this is the company that you really want to work for, examine the pros and cons again. If you have the nice "problem" of evaluating several job offers, ask for more time to make a proper decision. However, be realistic and considerate; taking weeks to decide is not recommended.

Negotiating the salary

As an intern, salary is not the top priority. The priorities are getting experience and building a network. For a new or recent graduate, it is still not the top priority, but it has more importance. As a graduate, you are no longer a student, and you should not settle for underpayment. If in doubt, it is perfectly okay to ask about the salary range for your position. Based on what other extra skills you have (foreign languages, programming, etc.), you can obviously demand to be placed at the higher end of the range.

Flexibility

New graduates are often surprised at how much flexibility there is in salaries. It is not unheard of or unusual for people doing identical jobs at a firm to have wildly different salaries. This can be due to when they started, who they know, tightness in the labor market, or their own assertiveness. Remember the old saying: "The open mouth gets fed." As many should know, your salary is only *one* aspect of your overall compensation. You should be aware of what other perks or benefits that are available. If the firm is generous, for example, in sponsoring further outside education or training, then a lower starting salary may be overlooked in the bigger picture. As you climb the corporate ladder, I suggest that your flexibility with salary becomes less.

Value vs. Hours

Working professionally in banking rarely involves getting paid by the hour. Yes, there are guidelines depending on your country, but in general, traders and investment bankers will work anywhere from 40 to 60 hours per week. I would like to advise you early in your career to focus on the *value* that you bring to a team versus how many hours you are there. There is a *big* difference between being busy and being productive. This old practice of racking up a crazy number of hours, hopefully, is on its way out, like the liquid lunch trend of the 1990's.

One team that I managed had a mom with a young child attending school, and she made it a practice of leaving early to get him from school every day. She approached me when she joined the team about the special need that she had. Honestly, I was hesitant at first, but she promised me exceptional performance. Bottom line, she turned out to be the team's top producer, and it should be no surprise that I also gave her the biggest bonus on our team. In reality, she made more money than I did.

Any serious manager will focus on the value that you bring and not so much on how many hours you hang around the office. This is something you should always remember, especially when it is salary or bonus negotiation time.

WAYNE WALKER

Making the most of the internship or student job

Now you have your internship, congratulations! Let us examine how to maximize your time in the position. The most obvious goal is to learn as much as you can, and you should. Especially paying attention to which types of behaviors get rewarded and which ones get punished. All along this process, you want to keep an open mind as much as possible and just soak up info. This open mind also means open to doing things that are not exactly in your job description. For example, on the trading team that I was a part of, due to the language skills of an intern working with us, at times, he helped execute trades. Not part of his job, but he was open, and in turn, we gave him extra training. To avoid any misunderstanding, this openness does not give the green light to unethical behavior.

Bottom line, an internship is way too early in the career exploration process to lock in exactly what you will want to do as a first job after you graduate.

Trust

As an intern or student employee, you are considered on the team but still a bit of an outsider. This I know from having worked with a few interns on the teams that I managed. In some cases, strangely enough, people might share or confess things to you that they would not with other regular team members. This is because, as an intern, you are kind of in a protected category. Your mistakes will be forgiven a lot faster and easier than others. The one mistake that will NOT be forgiven is to share, without permission, any confidential information that was given to you. Basically, you will have broken the trust, and depending who you did this with, your remaining days as an intern could be a living hell.

Market Making

One team that I often mention in class, when asked about where is one of the best departments or teams to join if your interest is in trading or the markets division of a bank, and that is market making. This is where you will learn a lot about interbank trading plus get deep insights on working an order book. This training will provide you with a solid base for just about any other department later. Market makers that I know have gone on to be heads of trading divisions, CEOs of mid-size brokers, and even head of sales.

Networking for interns

During your intern experience, no surprise, your goal, after learning practical skills, is networking and beginning to build professional contacts. These are the people who will recommend you for another internship or give you a contact with the people running the new graduate programs. From personal experience, a lot of the new traders hired were often employed prior as summer or winter interns. The feedback from students that I have taught in the GCMS classes is that many had their first jobs from internship connections.

A thing to keep in mind is that people in finance move around a lot, between companies and countries. Even though finance and investment banking are global, in reality, we know of each other way more than you would think just by observing from the outside. This is another reason to guard your reputation as you would your life. The friend or enemy made at one bank might be waiting for you at your next employer as a colleague, boss, or your boss's boss!

Europe and United States networking differences

Luckily, the differences are not that big, but the subtle differences matter. The importance of being of service to others first and making connections BEFORE you need them remains the same.

In America, walking up to strangers and connecting is not a big deal, and in New York City where I spent a lot of my career, that is almost expected. In Europe, especially in Northern Europe (Norway, Sweden, Denmark, Finland), people might consider this aggressive behavior. In London, things are a bit closer to New York style but with a little softer edge, depending on your circle. Therefore, for Americans, when in Europe, you should consider toning things down a bit if you are the upfront New Yorker type. For my European readers, when dealing with people from the United States, speak up, as the old saying goes: "The open mouth gets fed!"

WAYNE WALKER

The first job after graduation

Photo Notes: Not my first job after graduating from school, but I still network to this day with members of my old team. By the way, we are all now at different banks or have started our own firms.

I am the overly happy guy in the middle with outstretched arms.

"Real world"

Welcome to the "real world," as the cliché goes. The so-called real world is actually not so bad. The first good news is that you should be finally getting paid real money. A lot of what was suggested for interns can be applied to new graduates, but there is more urgency. Your skills acquisition and network building step up a few levels.

Skills acquisition, in practice, is that as soon as possible after your initial training is completed, you begin seeking additional training or, at the very least, let others know this is your wish. In most cases, your manager will view this positively. In many banks, the managers are rated on how well their teams progress. For example, if you manage a team where many people get promoted, that reflects positively on the manager. He or she is doing something right, plus it also makes that manager's team very attractive. Everyone will want to work there. Who would not want to work on a team where people progress?

Networking at the first job

The rules from the intern networking that were already covered apply, but we have refined things. What you will quickly notice once working on a trading desk is how many people have worked with each other at some point in their careers. This applies not only for traders, wealth managers, and market makers, but even the marketing teams have often had contacts from previous jobs.
One of your goals as the new team member is showing some flexibility and being open to doing favors, for example switching work schedules with a colleague if you work on a 24-hour desk. As covered before, this flexibility never includes unethical things. Being unethical will quickly catch up with you, and there goes your career.

In many firms, you will experience a certain amount of turnover in the staff. The people that you like, keep close ties with them as much as possible. They will become your news source for what is going on at other firms, plus you now have access to another network. You, in return, are their source of news at your firm or elsewhere. Another point to be aware of is that, as often as people leave firms, they can return to the same firm in a year or two!

WAYNE WALKER

The social scene

Many career books skip this part because it can be touchy. I am known for saying it like it is; therefore, I can do it. The trading and investment banking world, at times, seems like just one big party (outside of work). Several factors contribute to this; first, it is your well-paid salary. You will, in most cases, have a salary that allows you more entertainment room than the average person. In the case that you do not, no need to worry because there are so many company get-togethers. In Scandinavia, where I reside part of the year, there is a thing called "Friday bar" or "fredag bar" in Danish, where the banks or firms begin the party for you every Friday at the company premises. I can only say that I enjoyed all of my Friday bars without any incident. Unfortunately, I cannot say the same for all, especially those new to banking. You really need to be aware at these events; have fun yes, in fact have a lot of fun! However, with the alcohol, especially while still on your employer's property, I would remain on the conservative side.

At the company Christmas parties, I always tried to leave before things got too crazy. I was *no* angel. My friends and I took the extra partying *elsewhere*, away from the full view of all our colleagues that we would see Monday morning. Something for you to consider.

Dating at work

Dating on the job has happened at every place that I have ever worked. From my summer job as a camp counselor in New York during my university days to managing teams of bankers in Europe. During my time as an employee, I have seen quite a few people meet and end up married while at work, so there are some happy endings.

I suggest you do the on the job dating thing at your discretion. Some of the obvious no no's, dating your boss or harassing people for dates will not only get you fired or sued, but you might end up in criminal court defending yourself. Better idea is to date people outside of where you work. For full disclosure, I also dated where I worked, and when compared to dating outside of work, it just seemed dating outside of work was less complicated and stressful. In the end, you will have to see what works best for you, and in the current touchy legal environment, I would be very careful.

Thinking of hooking up in the middle of the workday? Resist the urge. The few times I heard of this happening while I was at work, it <u>always</u> ended badly for the people involved.

WAYNE WALKER

The GCMS Finance Assessment Exercise

This assessment exam was designed to give you some feedback on your knowledge of basic capital markets principles. The questions should make you think, but they should not be overly challenging since these are the basics. Most exams rarely give more than a minute per question; therefore, to be realistic, you should test yourself with that (one minute) as a benchmark. If you are having problems, then you should, of course, seek some practical training or books to help fill the gaps.

Please keep in mind that the full exams will usually have from 50 to 100 questions. This is only meant to be an "appetizer."

The GCMS Finance Assessment Exercise

1. Which of the following statements about savings behavior is most accurate?

(a) Expected increases in income encourage individuals to save less.
(b) Higher interest rates make individuals less willing to trade present consumption for future consumption.
(c) None of the above

2. Standard Deviation is a measure of
(a) Neither risk nor return
(b) Return
(c) Both risk and return
(d) Risk

3. A stock that is traded in the market with high volumes is called
(a) Liquid stock
(b) Illiquid stock
(c) Value stock
(d) Growth stock

4. Which one of the following is not a typical exit route for Private Equity Investor?
(a) IPO
(b) NCD
(c) Buy Back
(d) Strategic sale

5. When the Fed raises interest rates, what is the expected impact on Inflation?
(a) Decreases
(b) No impact
(c) Increases

6. What is the FOMC?

(a) Federal Official Market Corp
(b) Federal Office Market Committee
(c) Federal Open Market Committee

7. What does the CPI measure?

(a) Corporate pressure
(b) Inflation
(c) Consumer spending

8. Why are moving averages helpful as a trading tool?

(a) Studies show that it is better than other analysis tools.
(b) Gives perfect trade signals.
(c) Makes it easier to spot a trend.

9. Is it possible to trade forex during the week at 3 AM?

(a) Yes, the market is open 24/6.
(b) Yes, but only the Asian currencies.
(c) Only if approved by a senior dealer.

10. What is the purpose of a stop order?

(a) Stop the loss on a trade
(b) Stop the loss on a closed position
(c) To help new traders

11. When should a trader expect the most market volatility from a report?

(a) When the report is noticeably different from expectations
(b) When the report is as expected

(c) When the report is slightly different from expectations

12. What are examples of things that affect the forex market?

(a) Employment/job reports
(b) The number of newborns in Mexico
(c) How many view cable news this week

13. A model that describes the relationship between risk and expected return and is used in the pricing of securities is better known as

(a) Beta model
(b) Efficient market hypothesis
(c) Security market Line
(d) CAPM

14. Risk is measured by
(a) Volatility
(b) Interest rates
(c) Returns
(d) None of the above

15. A zero coupon bond will have zero _____ risk
(a) Reinvestment risk
(b) Interest rate risk
(c) Default risk
(d) Inflation risk

16. You are an international merchant who is doing business with Mexico. You will acquire a large number of pesos in the near future and you fear the value of the peso will decrease. How can you hedge your position?

(a) Sell peso futures contracts
(b) Sell dollar futures contracts

(c) Buy peso futures contracts
(d) None of the above

17. Johan expects 15,000 USD as a gift from his uncle. The money will be received in a month. He plans to invest 50% of his gift in shares. Recent trends in share prices indicate the share prices may go up. Upcoming elections may dampen the spirit of traders and if the government decides to adopt a stringent economic policy. Based on the information given, what should Johan do if he wants to benefit from the short time rally in stock prices?

(a) Buy long index futures/option
(b) Buy stocks from spot market by borrowing money
(c) Short sell index futures
(d) None of the above

18. The returns on Stock A and Stock B have a correlation coefficient of -1. When the price of Stock A appreciates by 12%, how will Stock B's price perform?

(a) Depreciate by 12%
(b) Appreciate by 12%
(c) Depreciate by 6.0%
(d) Stay unchanged

19. If a bond is selling at a premium
(a) Its coupon rate is below market rate.
(b) It is an attractive investment.
(c) Its realized compound yield will be less than the yield to maturity.
(d) Its current yield is lower than the coupon rate.

20. NASDAQ is
(a) The NASDAQ (acronym of National Association of Securities Dealers Automated Quotations) is an American stock exchange.
(b) A section of the NYSE where technology stocks are traded.
(c) The trading symbol for an aquatics company listed on the Amex.

The answer sheet is available at the end of the book.

GETTING THAT FIRST JOB OR INTERNSHIP IN FINANCE

Finance candidate interview questions

The interview questions presented are to be used as a heads-up of what to expect in a typical interview. You prepare best by formulating your answers to several versions of the questions in this guide. Either with a partner or on your own, you want to become as comfortable as you can with the TYPE of questions. This is all with the goal of making you as polished as possible.

Employers are looking for candidates with the following: Content, Practical, or Adaptive Skills.

- Content: Knowledge that is work specific, e.g., trading, language, coding, programming, etc.

- Practical Skills: Skills developed from past jobs or activities that the employer finds valuable, e.g., organizing, leading, developing, communicating, etc.

- Adaptive Skills: Personal characteristics such as being reliable, team player, self-motivated, punctual, etc.

What is the optimal strategy for answering these types of questions?

You must answer, with an overview of the task or problem, specific actions that you took and the end result of your actions. Your answer should contain all the following points.
Task: Our team was underperforming, higher than average trade errors.

Specific Action: I created and led training sessions to improve trade execution skills.
Result: We reduced trading errors by 50 percent.

Explanation of Choices

- Tell me about yourself and walk me through your CV. Give me a brief summary of your work history.
- Why did you choose your university?
- What courses did you do the best or worse in?
- Tell me about your college or graduate school experience.
- Why did you leave your last position?
- What did you learn about yourself at your last job?
- Tell me about your reasons for selecting this industry.
- Give examples of how you have used your greatest skills.
- What is your major weakness?
- What have been your major successes and accomplishments? How did you achieve these?
- What were your failures and what did you learn from them?
- Tell me your biggest regret.

Motivations

- What are your most significant achievements/accomplishments?
- What motivates you?
- What have been identified as your key strengths?
- What appeals to you about this position?

- What events have had an impact on your life?

- What kind of activities do you enjoy?

- Discuss something about yourself that I cannot learn from your CV.

- What would you do if you did not have to work for money?

- What do you do for fun?

- Where do you see yourself in 2-3 years?

Teamwork

- Describe a time when you were a member of a team that experienced difficulties. What did you do? What was the result?

- What specifically have you done to promote teamwork and cooperation among individuals and groups in a business situation? What was your motivation? How effective were your actions?

- Tell me about a manager you have worked with that you respect deeply. What are the characteristics of this person that make them effective and inspiring as the leader of a team?

- What role do you usually take in a team?

Dealing with uncertainty

- Tell me about a project you worked on that was constantly changing and unpredictable. How did you handle it?

- Describe a situation where you, or the people around you, were uncomfortable due to a lack of direction or guidelines. How did you react, and what were the results?

Initiative

- Provide an example of a time when you worked on a critical project/job with little or no supervision. How did you proceed? What was the result?

- What is the best example of how your initiative made the difference in achieving needed results?

- Describe a project in which you went beyond what was expected of you.

- What is the best example that you can provide of taking a calculated risk in an uncertain situation to go after a desired goal?

Relationship Building

- Describe an experience where you had to overcome strong resistance to your ideas or initiatives. Describe your audience, the nature of the issue you discussed with them, and the steps you took to influence the group.

- Recall a time when you persuaded others to do what you wanted.

- Provide the best example you can of how you worked successfully behind the scenes to influence an important business decision.

Leadership

- Provide an example of a situation where you were able to improve another person's performance. What led to the situation?

- Describe a situation where you had to take over supervision of an employee? What did you do?

- Give me examples of your leadership abilities.

- What would your team members say about you if I asked them for feedback on your leadership style?

Creativity

- Provide an example of when you spotted business opportunities to generate profits. How did you go about pursuing the opportunity? What was the outcome?

- Describe a situation when you suggested a creative approach to solving a problem. Was it accepted?

- Have you suggested a new idea to someone recently? What was the idea? What prompted the idea?

- What's the most creative/innovative thing you have ever done?

- Give me an example where you came up with a creative solution to a problem.

Integrity

- Tell me about a time when you made a promise that proved difficult to keep. What did you do to resolve the situation?

- Have you faced a situation where someone was not treated fairly? What did you do? What was the result?

- Tell me about a time you put the best interests of someone else ahead of your own. What went through your mind as you considered your decision? How did you feel about your choice?

Fast Learner

- Describe a time when you entered a new situation and quickly had to acquire knowledge to understand was happening. What tools did you use? What was the result?

- How do you respond to questions that involve content you are unfamiliar with?

Team and Culture

- Describe what would be an ideal environment for you.

- What do you enjoy most about the environment you currently work in? What aspects of your current job are you looking to avoid in your next job?

- What do you think this position requires, and how well do you match those requirements?

- Describe the most relevant and specific areas in your background that show you are qualified for this job.

- What matters most to you in your next position?

- How do you define stress, and how do you manage it?
- Why are you interested in this position?
- What is it about our company that interests you?
- Tell me about your reasons for selecting this industry.

The Close

- Why should we hire you?
- Why are you the ideal person for this position?
- What makes you different from the other candidates?
- Do you have any questions for me/us?

Resources

Some of my other books have been proven to help students and new graduates. By the way, several of them are also available in Spanish:

Algo Programming:

Expert Advisor Programming for Beginners: Maximum MT4 Forex Profit Strategies

Tech Analysis:

Technical Analysis for Forex Explained

Blockchain:

Blockchain: Real-World Applications and Understanding

Websites:

One of the better sites for job search and articles relating to investment banking and finance in general: https://www.efinancialcareers.com/

Practical capital markets education and career coaching:

https://www.gcmsonline.info/

Conclusion

Thank you for making it through to the end of *Getting That First Job or Internship In Finance.* Let's hope it was informative and able to provide you with the tools you need to achieve your goals of securing a finance job that challenges you! The next step is to practice the interview question until they become natural to you. For those that want to dive in even deeper, you can visit my website for other options.

Best of luck to you!

Profile of The Author

Wayne Walker is the director of a global capital markets education and consulting firm (gcmsonline.info). He has several years' experience leading and coaching teams of Investment Advisors and has managed top performing teams in the Private Client Group based on Bench Mark Earnings (BME). In addition, he is known for helping many with securing their first jobs in finance.

The GCMS assessment answer sheet

1 - A
2 - D
3 - A
4 - B
5 - A

6 - C
7 - B
8 - C
9 - A
10 - A

11 - A
12 - A
13 - D
14 - A
15 - A

16 - A
17 - A
18 - A
19 - D
20 - A

www.ingramcontent.com/pod-product-compliance
Lightning Source LLC
Chambersburg PA
CBHW030730180526
45157CB00008BA/3114